Conversational Hypnosis – A Practical Guide

By Michael Kiff

Michael Kiff is a professional writer, hypnotherapist and the author of *The Art of Influencing Others,* published by Define Success.

Define Success, Seattle 98087

ISBN-13: 978-1484991091

ISBN-10: 1484991095

Published by:

Define Success

15001 35th Ave W Suite 15-202 Lynnwood WA, 98087

http://bit.ly/DefineSuccessBooks

Disclaimer

While all attempts have been made to verify information provided in this publication, neither the author nor the publisher assumes any responsibility for the errors, omissions or contrary interpretation of the subject matter herein. Any perceived slights of specific persons, peoples or organization(s) is unintentional.

The purchaser or reader of this publication assumes responsibility for the use of these materials and information, including adherence to all applicable laws and regulations, federal, state and local. No guarantees of results are made. If you can't accept these terms, kindly return product. The Author and Publisher assume no responsibility or liability whatsoever on the behalf of any purchaser or reader of these materials.

Contents

Introduction

Conversational hypnosis, also commonly known as covert hypnosis, is the art of influencing others by giving them direct subconscious commands to follow that seem like normal everyday conversation. It is a style of communication that you will use to subtly direct anyone's subconscious mind to take action. When you practice the methods in this book you are going to be using hypnotic language patterns to influence others to take action and do what you want. It is not just what you are saying that is going to compel others to take action, it is a combination of how you say what you are saying. You are going to be learning how to use your voice, posture and body language in order to deliver a hypnotic command in a seemingly normal conversation that will influence the person you are talking to to take action. This is the art of conversational hypnosis.

When you use the hypnotic language patterns you are learning in this book, you can easily break down the walls of resistance and implant the desire to complete whatever action it is that you want them to take. If it is your desire, you can influence them to take action without them even understanding why they are doing what you want; they will just have a subconscious urge to do as you say.

One of the keys to effectively using conversational hypnosis is to convince the person you are persuading to believe that the action you are convincing them to take is a fun, safe and perfectly natural thing to be doing. You can convince anyone to do anything by delivering to them subtle hypnotic commands that assure them that the action is seamlessly normal and safe to do.

It is important that you find a way to make your command beneficial to the person that you are influencing. If you cannot find a way to make it beneficial then it is not a good command to be giving. I have made the mistake of influencing others to do something that is not in their best interest and believe me when I say that it is not good for anyone. There are always consequences to using hypnosis on others. If you make someone else feel bad about anything for whatever reason, they would resent you for it and possibly want revenge. It is better for everyone if you use the techniques that you will be learning in this book to benefit others because it will also benefit you.

The truth is that anyone can be persuaded and influenced to do anything that you want them to; so it is in your best interest to put yourself in the mind-set that this is the truth. You will discover, as you carry on reading this entire book, an assortment of methods that you can use to do this swiftly and without difficulty.

Why Hypnosis?

Hypnosis is communication with the subconscious mind. The reason that you want to communicate with the subconscious mind is that it is easier to convince than the conscious mind. Conversational hypnosis is the art of communicating with the subconscious mind in everyday conversation. Therefore, with this book you are learning to speak to a person's subconscious mind because doing this will make it really easy for you to convince and influence others.

As you follow along you are going to be learning how to influence the subconscious mind by using your voice tone and inflection. The subconscious mind is very responsive to changes in voice tone and with the proper inflection you make your voice hypnotically stimulating. This is what you are learning before you move on to other aspects, such as the psychological devices, because you need to know how to make everything that you say convincing.

Once you start the development of creating your proper hypnotic tone of voice, you will then find that you have the ability to make everything you say convincing; which will allow you to move on to the psychological devices – which are methods or points that you will specifically use in order to inject your command into the persons subconscious.

I call these psychological devices *points* because they are like arrow points that you shoot into the other person's brain. You can also think of them as the point of a hypodermic needle that you use to inject your commands directly into the person's subconscious mind. I use my hypnotic voice to insert these points into the other person with confidence that they are working to influence because I know the signs to look for and experience the successful results. You are going to be learning the signs to look for that will give you the confidence that your commands have worked too.

As you can now tell, the conversational hypnosis that you learn in this book is one of the best ways in which to persuade and influence others because it bypasses the conscious mind in order to directly influence the subconscious mind to take action. Consequently, learning hypnosis is the easiest way to gain the power of persuasion and influence over others.

The Most Powerful Tool

If you have ever wanted to know what the most powerful tool to influence and persuade others is, then you need to know that it is the ability to use conversational hypnosis effectively; because, in order to convince anyone to do anything you need to know how to persuade them instantly. This can only be done by bypassing their conscious mind, which will almost always try to contradict what you are saying, and speak directly to their subconscious mind – which is much more open to suggestion.

You will not have any influence at all over anyone if you do not cultivate the ability to compel them to want to listen to you and do as you say. This can only happen when you work your way through their walls of resistance. The easiest way to do that is to bypass these walls and communicate directly to their subconscious mind.

Look, I am going to be revealing to you, in this book, how to show others that they want to follow your lead. When you focus on communicating directly to their subconscious mind they will easily be convinced to follow you. They will want to listen to what you say because you are bypassing their conscious mind and talking directly to their subconscious. When you push aside their defense and open the door to their lower levels of thought, you will easily convince them to do as you wish.

Where to Begin

If you want to become a master at conversational hypnosis, you should read this book from front to back in its entirety; because it is set up to teach you with a gradual process that leads you into becoming an expert. You may skip ahead to learn some tricks that will actually work for you, but you will not master hypnosis and your skills will be rudimentary at best. Hypnosis is something that does take some time, practice and dedication. Once you have mastered conversational hypnosis by using all the information that is found in this book, you will have a power of influence over others that is unbeatable.

Ask yourself this question, "would I rather become a master persuader and have unbeatable conversational hypnosis skills or just learn some quick tricks that may work some of the time?" I think that mastering conversational hypnosis and becoming an unbeatable persuader is the better choice. When you read and follow *all* of the information in this book you will become a master at conversational hypnosis. If you decided to skip ahead and learn some quick tricks you would experience only minimal success.

So, the best way to use this book is to read every single page and do the exercises because when you do you are going to be so much more powerful than the other person who just inactively reads the material without doing the exercises. When you read every page, and actually practice using all the methods in this book, you will come to realize all of the advantages of following this manual word for word; you will start to see that you are becoming a master of conversational hypnosis with unstoppable power over someone who just uses the tricks, and especially all the others who don't even do that much.

You may ask, "why it is important to follow the entire book if learning some quick tricks will work to influence others?" Because by practicing everything in this book you're gaining powerful knowledge now and you really begin to understand that you have to follow a specific formula that includes more than just learning hypnotic speech patterns. You see, what the majority of people don't comprehend is that your body language has to be a certain way, your voice has to be projected in a certain way, your thoughts and eye contact need to be just right, and jumping ahead to learn just the tricks isn't going to give you the power that following along and practicing everything in this book is giving you. When you follow along, page by page, practice all the methods you are learning, and as you master every technique that you are learning along the way; you easily begin to understand why you are doing it –

because your persuasion skills begin improving by leaps and bounds.

Do you understand? I think that it is quite clear and hope you succeed with this book because it has everything that you need to know about mastering conversational hypnosis. I know that you will succeed if you follow each exercise given.

Gain an Understanding

The way in which this book is laid out is very logical, and as you continue to read you will find out why it is best to learn and practice the methods in this book in the order that they are presented – which is as follows:

-First, you learn exactly how all of life is controlled and manipulated, and how you can easily become the one who is in control.

-Second, you will learn exactly how to put yourself in the right mind frame to make others feel more comfortable around you, so that they are more willing to do as you say. You are going to be building rapport with everyone that you come in contact with so that they enjoy being around you so much that they want to help you with anything that you desire. A lot of time and energy is spent on this because one of the most important keys to making people want to do as you say is to make them feel like you are on their side and want to help them.

-Third, you are going to learn how to soften people up in order to get them to talk about personal subjects that they normally would consider private and not want to discuss. This is important in order to get them to trust you more, and also lets you know more about them, so that you can effectively persuade them by incorporating their interests and experiences.

-Fourth, you are going to learn the basic special formula that makes up the fundamentals of conversational hypnosis. This is where you learn how to give others a direct command that seems like normal conversation so that they don't notice it is a command, but they will pick it up with their subconscious mind, actually want to follow it, and they do it without even thinking of why.

-Next, you will learn how to build your hypnotic voice. The subconscious mind is very receptive to changes in tonality and inflection of one's voice. When you master your hypnotic voice it is going to increase the power of your conversational hypnosis abilities 10-fold. Part of what you are learning with this is the correct posture, breathing, and enthusiasm to make what you say more compelling.

-After that, you are learning the complete hypnotic process. This is the exact hypnotic formula that you will always use in order to effectively lead anyone to do as you say. This is the complete process that makes up conversational hypnosis. At this point, you have already learned the basics and will be structuring your own hypnotic pattern.

-Then, it is time to learn how to put people into trance states in order to amplify your commands and make them more open to suggestion. The few people who do not want to do as you suggest at first will easily do as you suggest after you have effectively put them into a trance state.

-Finally, you will learn the psychological devices, or hypnotic language patterns that I call hypnotic points. These are specific methods that you use that have been proven to work to effectively inject a command directly into the person's subconscious mind. These are the tricks that many people use with success to influence others; however, they are extremely more powerful after you have mastered everything else in this book. The way that I look at it is like this: you can bake a cake by following a recipe without really learning how to cook. This is like using these psychological devices without learning how to hypnotize someone. On the other hand, you can take the time and learn how to cook. Then, you can make a cake with your knowledge and change the ingredients if you like because you know what ingredient does what. This is like learning everything that is in this book. Once you have read this book and mastered conversational hypnosis you will be able to switch everything up, create your own hypnotic patterns, and be able to change your technique in order to adapt to any situation.

Life is Controlled

Unfortunately for most people, the world is set up for the masses to be controlled. From the very young age of about 6-8 years old you began to be programmed to follow someone else's lead. You were trained to perform the proper tasks of life that someone else has laid out for you. You were trained to get up and go to school every morning at the same time. After you arrived at school, you would sit in a classroom and memorize the supposed facts that were being given you, do the work that the teacher gave you, follow everything the teacher said, and worst of all – you were told exactly what you should think. Unless you were lucky enough to have parents who taught you otherwise, you were never taught how to think for yourself.

This pattern is forced upon you all throughout school, even throughout all of the University levels. Then, once you graduate into "the real world" you do the exact same thing. You get up and go to work every morning at the same time, you perform memorized tasks that were given to you from someone of authority, told exactly how you should act, given what to think, and worst of all – you can even be punished for doing things your own way and thinking for yourself. You are highly discouraged and kept from gaining any real power for fear that you may end up taking it from someone else.

There are very few cases of individuals actually being taught to think for themselves and encouraged to be creative in their line of work. This is a shame, because it is proven that companies who encourage and stimulate creative thought actually end up becoming an extremely highly-valued company – with employees that are very sought after, and an overall company value that cannot be matched. This may seem obvious to some, but the truth is that most of those who hold any sort of power are in great fear of losing it; so they encourage the manipulation of the masses into being individuals who not only just do what their told, but actually prefer to follow someone else's lead.

Just by understanding the fact that the world is set up for the majority of people to follow the leader, you have taken the first step that is necessary in order for you to succeed at conversational hypnosis. Conversational hypnosis is about covertly leading others into doing what you want. You now understand that the vast majority of people are already conditioned to follow the leader. You can easily become that leader, and everyone that you come in contact with will actually want to do as you say; because they are so used to following the leader, that it will be too uncomfortable and difficult for them not to.

Just by understanding that the world is set up for you to follow the leader actually gives you the foundation for success in becoming the leader. By understanding how the world works, you can choose to be a leader and not succumb to others who appear to be in charge. When you master the conversational hypnosis techniques in this book, you are actually able to influence the people who seem to have the most power, because they most likely have only learned how to be persuasive; while you are going to

9

convince them, unconsciously, to believe that they are the ones who came up with the idea of doing what you want in the first place.

There are many instances of salesman, celebrities, and those in power using subconscious "tricks" in order to get you to do what they want. You only need to flip on the T.V. in order to see several cases on every channel at any given moment. The thing that is interesting is that they usually are just using tricks that they learned in order to move ahead, and don't even understand what it is that they are doing. As you sit there and read this book, you are actually learning the truth about conversational hypnosis, and will never be fooled by their tricks again. You are learning a way to influence almost everyone without having to use simple tricks, because you are learning the reason why those tricks work. Once you understand the reason behind something, you can easily change it to suit your needs because you know why it works in the first place. So, stick with it and keep reading because you are becoming the master of persuasion that cannot be beat.

Now that you realize the truth, don't you think that it is silly that the supposed established facts are taken without argument? Nobody ever truly has power over anyone else unless they give them power. Those who are in charge have just learned to convince people that they are right. Whenever someone decides to argue with them, the argumentative person is just punished, which further enforces the authority's power.

Hence, it is quite obvious that if most people are conditioned to follow the leader (and even forced to do so in many cases), and if you were to reproduce the exact same hypnotic tools, you could easily become the leader and control almost anyone that you come in contact with.

As a matter of fact, once you have finished reading this entire book, you can easily see that you have more power than they do, because you can plainly see through their very child-like tricks, and you will know that you can always do better because you fully understand what they are doing. After you have finished reading this book you will always know that you can do it better.

I know that if you are still reading this: you are serious about mastering conversational hypnosis, and want to get started on learning the specific tools that you use to successfully influence anyone to do what you want. There is just one more thing that you will want to fully understand before we move on; so, if you would, please follow along while I explain why hypnosis works so well, and you learn the secret that keeps you in control.

People almost always seek external authorities in order to solve their problems. Read that again because it is important. Think about it, if you have a headache you go for the pain reliever (like aspirin) because someone told you that it cures your headache. The aspirin itself is an outside authority that you are seeking in order to solve your headache problem. If you are tired you may go for the coffee or other caffeinated beverage in order to give you a bit of a boost. If you don't understand something, you will seek out and external authority in order to help you understand it. If your car is broken down you will probably take it to a mechanic. If you need money, you are most likely going to go to the bank. The list goes on and on. If you are bored you may turn on the T.V. or pick up a book. It seems as if it is just the way that the world works.

The reason that this is so important to understand is that it is one of the biggest reasons why conversational hypnosis works. People are always seeking answers, and always looking for other people to fix their problems. A lot of the time, a person does not even know that they have a problem until someone else tells them that it is a problem. Then they go looking for an outside authority to fix their problem.

Again, this is big. As you read these words you may be having a big light go off in your head. People are always looking for an outside authority and you can easily become that authority. An authority is what you are learning to become with conversational hypnosis, because, when you use the tools in this book, you are influencing the person you are talking to, through their subconscious mind, to follow your instructions; which is what the person wants to do anyway.

Mind Frame and Rapport

After reading the last chapter, you have started to have the right mind frame for conversational hypnosis; because you understand that it is easy to lead the thoughts of others, since most people need an external authority, and you can easily become that authority. Now, in this chapter, you are going to further prepare yourself to gain the trust of others, put yourself more into the proper mind frame for successfully persuading others, and learn how to properly build rapport with all those you come in contact with. In other words, you are going to learn how to purposefully give off a "good vibe" to everyone that you come in contact with: so they naturally trust you more, and are more open to suggestion because they let down their guard.

First off, you have to be in the right mind frame to properly persuade others to subconsciously let down their guard. You need to purposefully direct your thoughts in order to give the impression that you are only trying to help the other person.

Have you ever just had a really bad feeling about someone, and not trusted them even though they seemed to be perfectly harmless? I am sure that this has happened on many occasions because the subconscious mind picks up on everything that comes from another person. The subconscious mind picks up on all six senses (including thought) and notices even the minutest detail.

Why is this important? Because in order to effectively use conversational hypnosis you need most everyone you come in contact with to trust you and let down their guard so that they are more receptive to your suggestions. This means that you have to "give a good vibe" or, in other words, you need to be in the right mind frame that gives them the proper subconscious cues that you are to be trusted. More specifically, when you are talking with someone and using conversational hypnosis, you are obviously not going to be thinking, "You are so stupid and I am so smart using conversational hypnosis on you." Instead, you need to be thinking thoughts similar to, "isn't it really fun to talk with me and more interesting then talking with most people."

You can look at it another way: in order for other's to see that they should follow you, you need to show them that you can be trusted. People will never follow (at least not for long) someone that they do not trust. The best way to gain people's trust is by always thinking about how following you is beneficial; because when you think about helping the other person it will show in all of your senses, and they will subconsciously pick up on that.

People love to have fun, so think about how fun this is. You are reading this book because you want to master conversational hypnosis, which is fun when you make it fun, so think about that and you should be fine. Obviously, this does not mean, "hee, hee I am doing this to you" which is selfish. It is more like, "isn't this fun!" which is mutual enjoyment. Do you understand? I think that it is really clear, so I know that you understand enough to go on.

So, now that you know what frame of mind you are in, it is time to gain even more rapport and trust. With me, I understand that rapport is the most important key to persuading others. Just to be clear, rapport is a term used to express the relationship of two or more people who are in sync or on the same wavelength as each other; since they feel very similar or relate well to each other. Clearly, when you gain rapport, like with me now, you are gaining a friend who is on the same wavelength, and will trust you more. So, you can easily see how this makes it much easier for you to persuade anyone you talk with to follow your commands.

After you have read this chapter in its entirety, and you have mastered rapport, anyone you converse with will let down their walls, let your subconscious commands right in, and they will do as you say without any struggle.

Does this sound way too good to be true?

It isn't. By using the right tools that you are learning in this chapter you easily give everyone the 'vibe' that you are to be trusted. They easily feel like they are similar to you and enjoy talking with you. You have already learned the right mind-frame and now the rest is easy. You just have to be willing to be flexible with your thoughts and actions; then you can willingly change them to give off the subconscious signals that you are top notch.

Think about it, have you ever had the opportunity to meet someone who you almost instantly felt comfortable around? Yes, you are sure to have experienced this because everyone has. This is because you are picking up on the subconscious signals that tell you it is all right. You are learning to purposefully give these signals off.

Remember, you have already learned how to have the right state of mind. The rest of it has to do with sound, sight, smell, taste and touch. Everyone else is going to be sending

14

random subconscious signals that are either positive or negative. You are using self-control in order to send all positive signals. When you do this they can not help but think, "I just have this great feeling about you!"

To begin with, you have to appear to be a leader. You have to give the gestures of a leader, have the tone of a leader, look like a leader, and yes even smell like a leader. A leader does not smell like week-old garbage. When you act and appear to be a leader it makes it much easier for others to follow your subconscious commands, because you already are letting them know that you are a leader by your appearance and actions.

Here are the actions of a leader:

-Keep your shoulders back and spine straight. A leader never slouches and always holds the head up high.

-Keep proper eye contact. ***IMPORTANT NOTE*** A leader never stares for prolonged periods of time because it makes people feel uncomfortable. This is important because all too many people think that they need to give the penetrating stare in order to show others who is boss. This never works, it only makes people uncomfortable and not want to be around you. Always look people in the eye frequently, remember to blink and keep a steady gaze that stays above the chin. Smiling, listening, and thinking fun thoughts will always show in the eyes.

-Your speech patterns should reflect power. Speak with a tone that is deep and resonant, always end sentences in a downward reflection, and always pause after something important is said to give it more importance.

-Your movements are to be grand and sweeping. The leader has a presence by standing tall, holding the shoulders back, chin high, speaking with a resonating voice that demands attention, and using large motions that cannot be missed. When listening, the leader's hands are to be held behind the back because this gives the subconscious signals of leadership. Hands are always to be kept away from the face. Do not ever cross the arms because it sends the subconscious signal that you are closed off; which tends to persuade the other person to be closed off to you as well.

Now that you are giving off the impression that you are a leader by your actions, you need to further persuade others to follow you by building more rapport. This is easily done once you realize that people are primarily interested in their own benefit. It is human nature, and now that you know it – you can use this to your advantage.

I am sure, as you look around, you can see that people are interested in their own self-interest first. It is no big secret, but as you read on, you will see how powerful this knowledge is when used to your advantage. Most people like to pretend that they are not primarily interested in their own benefit, mainly because they do not want to appear selfish. Once you have accepted this fact, you can easily gain rapport over anyone you converse with by skillfully gearing the conversation towards their own personal interests. They will love to talk to you because you are talking about what they love and are excited about most.

This is a very easy thing to do. All you have to do is ask them questions about their lives and talk about them. Always gear the conversation towards them by talking about their: interests, hobbies, days, family, etc. Just ask questions like:

-How was your day?

-Did you have fun on your days off (or vacation, break, trip, etc.)?

-How is your family?

-What do you think about _____?

I think you get the point. People truly do not care how interesting you think something is – they just care how interesting that *they* think it is. The secret is to get them to talk about themselves and their interests, and then they will think you are the most excellent conversationalist around.

Now that you have learned to take on the appearance of a leader, so others will *want* to follow you, and how to get people interested in talking with you by persuading them to talk about themselves; it is time to gain even more rapport by using more covert methods of influence, which you will learn as you read on.

It is quite normal to get excited over this, because it really is so exciting. So go ahead, get excited. It is ok. You are going to love me for this! Because, in the next few paragraphs, you are going to learn how to make people love you even more. The more that they love you, the more that they *want* to do as you say.

First off, you must get people to feel as important as possible. When you make a person feel important enough, they feel so good that they do almost anything for you. Entire wars are fought and won because the people fighting in them were convinced that what they are doing is important. When you make people feel important, they will fight to talk with you any chance they get! This is simply because they *feel so good* when they are around you. Everyone has a deep seated need to feel like they matter.

So how do I make people feel important?

1. **Listen to them**. The power of listening to another person is so amazing that this alone can get them to think you are the most interesting person ever. I have heard time and time again about how great it is to talk with me when I hardly

said a word other than, "That is so (interesting, funny, sad, weird, etc.), tell me more!" People are so used to waiting for their turn to talk that, when you truly listen to them, they can't help but feel important, because you are showing them that what they say actually matters.

2. **Compliment them**. Sincere compliments will always make a person feel more important. This can only be done when you pay attention to them. Insincere, generic compliments are never well received and will get you nowhere. When you pay attention, you can easily compliment them on some action they took that you admire, or something new that they are wearing. The funny thing is, when people love talking with you, they will just come up and tell you things that they are proud of, and then you can simply compliment them about it.

3. **Use their names**. People feel important whenever you use their names. However, it is obvious that a lot of other people have taken this tip to the extremes when they talk to you. I am sure you have noticed these people – it is quite apparent when they are throwing your name around in unnatural places, all over their sentences. I am sure you have experienced this, and know what I mean. When using their names, just use it naturally. You can use their name when you great them, say goodbye, or ask them a questions. It does not have to be a lot.

Examples:

"Hello, Tom. Nice to see you again. How is it going?"

"Look forward to seeing you again next week, Tom."

"You know Tom, that reminds me, how is your kid doing with his soccer?"

As you can see, this is using Tom's name naturally. I do not know why so many people (especially salesman) have taken to throwing your name in whenever and wherever they can. This is not natural, is really obvious, and does nothing towards gaining rapport.

4. **Show people that what they say is important.** You are already doing this by listening to them, but you can also say things like, "oh really" or "is that so" when they say something interesting. Do this with enthusiasm. Also, when they are done with a sentence and it is your turn to talk, pause for just a second before answering them. This gives them the impression that what they just said is important and worth thinking over. They will pick up on this subconsciously. It also gives you a moment to think about what you are going to say next. Sometimes I pause for a moment and then even say something like, "huh, it is interesting that you said that. I think…" I think that you understand.

5. **If someone is waiting for you acknowledge them.** All it takes is a second to let them know that you will be with them in a moment.

6. **When talking with a group, talk to everyone.** Switch from person to person, making eye contact with everyone equally. Always try and use everyone's name at least once if possible.

Get them to like you

Now that you have learned a few strategies to make people feel important, it is time to learn some amazing covert techniques that you can use to get anyone to like you instantly. When you use these techniques, your power over others is going to be so persuasive that they think you are the most awesome person to talk to, and they will strive to be around you as much as possible because you get along so well.

Technique Number One:

Talk like they do – More specifically, talk at the same speed, utilize the same tempo, and use the same tone, words and speech patterns as they do. This does not mean that you have to attempt a southern drawl if you are not from the south – that will most likely just irritate them. Instead, just talk at the same pace, tone, and volume that they do, and use similar words.

If someone obviously never uses big words, don't try to impress them with you knowledge of the dictionary.

Another part of this is speaking in the same terms as they think. You do not have to read their mind, just listen to what they say. People think in terms of visual, auditory, kinesthetic, olfactory (smell), and gustatory (taste) representations. Usually one is more prominent than all the rest.

So, if someone says something like, "I see what you mean." You are going to want to speak in more visual terms so that they can relate better. For example, "you can see how useful this is." If someone says something like, "yeah, I hear ya." You would use auditory terms like, "listen to this…" and so forth.

In order to help you out, and give you an idea of what language pattern someone is thinking in most, so that you can use the proper style; here are some of the words that people say, listed under the proper terms:

Visual - see, look, foggy, clear, bright, picture, view, imagine, sight for sore eyes, focused, reveal, dawn, illuminate, hazy, an eyeful, take a peek, short sighted

Auditory - tell, hear, sound, listen, silence, hush, tune in, resonate, loud and clear, rings a bell, melody, hush

Kinesthetic - feel, touch, grasp, hard, concrete, unfeeling, get hold of, catch on, tap into, scrape, solid, pull some strings, make contact

Olfactory (smell) - fishy, stale, putrid, scented, fresh, smoky, nosy

Gustatory (taste) - bitter, sour, sweet, tasty, juicy, salty, yummy

These are just a few of the many words that people will use often in their sentences, which will give you a clue as to which primary language terms they think in. As you can see, the more you listen to people, the better you are able to influence them.

So, when you are talking with someone, and you are using the same representational patterns that they think in, talking in the same tone, at the same speed, at the same tempo, and using similar words that they use; they are now relating to you tremendously and are extremely more open to your subconscious suggestions.

Technique Number Two:

Mirror their gestures – When someone puts their hand on their chin you have about 30 seconds to do something similar, and they will subconsciously pick up on it. This sends the signal that you are like them and they will naturally feel closer to you.

Remember that we are building rapport here, right now, and the more comfortable someone feels around you, and the more that they relate to you, the more they are going to be open to all of your suggestions.

Notice that your gesture only has to be *something similar* within about 30 seconds. So if they touch their chin, you have about 30 seconds to put your hand to your face somewhere.

Another benefit of doing this, is that it will bring your attention to what kind of gestures they make when they have certain emotional states – like getting excited. This can be a gold mind of information because you can use the same gesture when you want them to get excited about taking action and doing what you suggest – subconsciously or otherwise.

Do you see how useful this information is? Yes, it is simple; BUT IT WORKS!

Technique Number Three:

Breathe with the person – When you are matching the person's breathe it sends the subconscious signal that you are on the same wave length. This makes it easier to match their tempo and speed too.

Another advantage to this is that when you are speaking, it seems to their subconscious like they are the one who is saying what you are saying because you are taking a breath at the same time in between words. When you do this, it matches their internal dialogue and they think that what you are saying is exactly what they are thinking in the first place.

Just try it for yourself and you will find out how powerful this actually is. The ease of these powerful techniques is amazing and they work tremendously because they are based on building a great relationship. Now, with me, I look at it like an enjoyable game that we are both playing.

Technique Number Four:

Pretend that you are that person – Do not do this when they are right in front of you because they may think that you are mocking them. But when you are alone and have some spare time, pretend like you are them. Do things as they would do: talk as they would talk, walk as they would walk, and act as they would act.

When you take the time to pretend like you are someone an amazing thing happens: you naturally get more of an understanding of what it is like to be them. Of course they are going to feel like they can trust you when it is so obvious that you understand them so well. Others cannot help but feel more like you when you actually take the time to get to know them so intimately.

Remember that the building rapport techniques you have learned so far are extremely important to the conversational hypnotic process because building rapport with all those you communicate with is essential if you want them to open up to you and actually do your subconscious commands.

Soften Them Up

A big reason that you build rapport with a person is to help them feel more comfortable around you, so that they are more receptive to suggestion. A big part of the hypnotic suggestion that you will be using on them involves asking very personal questions, in order to get them excited about what they are talking about, so that you can use that excitement in order to get them excited about helping you. People are willing to talk about the most intrusive subjects when you have built enough rapport. However, this is much easier done when you soften them up first.

Let me explain…

When you are talking to someone, and you just start in on them with the asking of personal questions about their likes and dislikes, you may get opposition because it can seem intrusive. The way to get around this is to use softener lines to begin with that puts them in the right frame of mind in order to answer your otherwise intrusive questions. For example, before I begin to really lead a person into an excited state by talking about their desires, I always start by saying something like, "I hope that you are not freaked out by this or anything, but I am a bit of a dork, and I am really curious as to what your interests are, so I would like to get to know a little more about you, is that alright?" I shake my head yes when I ask if it is ok. I then move on to using hypnotic patterns on them with ease because they have let down their guard.

Now, it is really difficult for someone to object to anything you say when you soften them up first, and doing so also makes using conversational hypnosis much easier.

Here are some other softener lines:

-Would you mind if I asked you a weird question, just for fun?..

-I know this might seem a bit strange, but just for the sake of the interesting conversation we are having…

-I just have to say, and I hope that you do not find this too weird or anything, but…

These are just a few examples of softener lines that you can use in order to get away with saying almost anything. These all work very well because they diminish any possible objection that they would have had in following your lead and suggestions.

You can also soften them up substantially by using a lot of 'fluff talk' that naturally leads into them getting excited enough for you to begin your hypnotic patterns on them.

You need to use a lot of fluff talk in order to appear to be having a normal conversation, while secretly using hypnotic suggestions on them, or else it will not seem normal and your suggestions will not work.

With fluff talk, you will always be guiding the person towards talking about feelings, so that they get excited, and then you can move on to your hypnotic patterns. You will understand how to use fluff talk and easily transfer into hypnotic patterns with an example here:

"What did you do over the weekend?"

"Oh, nothing really: just stayed home and watched T.V."

"Yeah, I like watching T.V… it is real fun sometimes isn't it."

"I suppose.."

"What is your favorite show?"….

I think you get the point. You have to always gear them towards talking about something that excites them, makes them happy, or any other good feelings. *The most important aspect to using fluff talk is to get them talking about good feelings.*

Once they start to get excited about something, you merely have to keep talking about it, and show enthusiasm about it yourself, because when you do this you will always be building rapport with them, and then you can easily begin using your subconscious persuasion. All of this is so easy that I am sure you can see that you are going to be able to do everything in this book with little effort. It is so fun once you practice it in the real world.

Now that you understand that people actually want to follow someone else's lead and you can easily become that leader, that conversational hypnosis is the most powerful tool in order to become that leader, and how

to build rapport and soften them up in order to get them more receptive to accept your hypnotic suggestions; it is time for you to learn the basic hypnotic formula.

The Basic Hypnotic Formula

Before you learn the psychological devices known as hypnotic points, it is important for you to learn the basics of the hypnotic process; so right now I am giving you the basic hypnotic formula that you will use in all of your conversational hypnosis. This is the technique that you will always use in order to covertly compel others to do as you say.

This is the basic formula that you will use with any hypnotic methods that you find in this book. In other words, there are many methods that you will use this basic formula with. This is the base formula that you will use to deliver your hypnotic commands into a person's subconscious brain. With this formula you can use it for any hypnotic method you choose in order to get great results that work naturally.

Basically, in this chapter you are learning how to properly send an embedded command into anyone's mind with your conversational skills, and with this embedded command comes the results that you want.

The art of this conversational hypnosis that you are learning right now is to put an embedded command into a sentence that seems like a normally innocent part of a conversation, but is really covert hypnotic instruction that anyone you speak with naturally follows subconsciously. This is only achieved with the following basic hypnotic formula.

The Formula is: a precise set of words (trick phrases), followed by an action verb that presumes you (the person you are hypnotizing), and then the hypnotic command.

It's that simple!

The precise sets of words you will be using are known as "trick phrases" and are also in the chapter called "trick phrases". When you say one of these trick phrases followed by an action verb (for example: feel, do, begin, give, etc.), and then a command; you have now communicated to the subconscious mind and delivered hypnotic instruction. It is so easy!

It is important for you to keep your commands uncomplicated, so that they are easy to follow, because the subconscious mind can only process simple commands. Simple commands that are straight and to the point, like "feel better now", are much better than complicated commands, like "feel like your sickness is going away and you are getting better." You want to make it easy for the subconscious mind to follow what you are telling it to do, so it can easily do what you want; so, keep your commands simple and easy to follow.

Some of the best concepts in the world are always the simplest, because the simplest solutions will always be the easiest for us to make happen. If you are an alcoholic and were to quit drinking, it is so much easier and more powerful for you to *just quit drinking*. That is also the simplest way. Sometimes people love to make it harder on themselves by using medications, rehabs, or other difficult methods.

As you can see, the hypnotic formula that you are using in all of the hypnotic methods found in this book is really simple and easy to follow. I am telling you this so that you now know that it is very easy to successfully use conversational hypnosis. So keep it simple and you will always succeed.

This is just the hypnotic formula, and it needs to be used with a hypnotic method that you will be learning in this book as well, so just remember that conversational hypnosis is very easy to use when you keep it simple, and everyone will always do as you say.

As far as hypnotic methods go, you will be learning several in this book. We will go over in great detail exactly how to hypnotize anyone, anywhere, and anytime. Just remember that you use this basic hypnotic formula in all of these methods, because you always need it in order to succeed.

Your Hypnotic Voice

Developing you hypnotic voice is a very important step in the process of mastering conversational hypnosis; so, do not skip this chapter because it is your voice that will tell your subject's subconscious mind that you are giving it a command. When you use your voice correctly, with confident persuasion that reflects a downward tonality, you are perceived by the subconscious mind to be making a command. This happens even when, on the surface, you appear to be just talking normally and having a normal conversation.

Have you ever talked to a young lady, or anyone else for that matter, that always ends their statements in an upward tonality? On a daily basis, I am sure, because a lot of people talk in this fashion. The problem with this way of speaking is that it tells everyone, at least subconsciously, that the person who is speaking is always asking a question, this is perceived to be because they are unsure of themselves and need guidance. When a sentence is ended in an upward tonality, it sends the signal that help is needed, because the person appears to be asking a question.

When you are using conversational hypnosis, and sending commands for the person to follow, you do not want to give your command with an upward tonality because they will not follow your apparent question.

Now, there are exceptions to this rule. When it comes to talking with a very dominant male figure, especially when you are a woman, giving your commands with a downward tonality will not work. Some men do not like being told what to do, especially by women. These men will actually respond better to commands that appear to be questions, because their minds will let down their natural defense to being told what to do. I have yet to find a woman who responds better in this way, but it is possible.

If you find that a person with a more dominant personality is not responding to your commands, or worse, responding to your commands with violent opposition; simply change the commands to be given with an upward reflection. In this way, you appear to be taking a more passive role, while actually convincing their subconscious mind to do what you say.

Have you ever talked with someone who usually speaks and ends their sentences in a very monotone way? Yes, this can be quite boring; but it also sends the message, at least to the subconscious mind, that the person is merely making a statement, not a question or command. This may be exactly why we usually find monotone speech patterns so boring, because they are not asking us a question or giving us a command; they are not engaging us in conversation. Statements and facts are fine when mixed up with other types of conversation, but alone they just overwhelm the brain with too much apparently statistical information.

When you are using conversational hypnosis, you do not ever want to give your commands with a monotone voice, because nobody will do as you say. They will inevitably think that you are just making statements that bear no action on their part.

Now, you can turn any comment (even a question) into a command by giving it with a downward inflection. When you say to someone, "isn't this fun?" with a downward inflection it actually turns this question into a command that is telling them that it is fun.

When you are using conversational hypnosis, you usually want to give your commands with a downward inflection, so that it sends a signal to the other persons subconscious that you are telling it to do something. The only exception is when speaking with a very aggressive individual that will respond better to the more passive upward inflection.

In addition to using the proper inflection when giving your commands, you are going to want to alter your voice when the command is spoken. You will either raise or lower your voice, and speak more slowly in order to give the command a more hypnotic effect. This tells the other person's subconscious mind that this part of the sentence is different and needs to be paid attention to.

When you master the skill of properly embedding commands into your sentences, by slightly changing their volume, and ending with the proper downward or sometimes upward inflection; **you have more hypnotic influence than most people and gain obedience effortlessly**, because most people consciously perceive your commands as mere statements, while subconsciously following your commands. The typical person will always automatically follow your suggestions without even thinking about it, because they are receiving them as subconscious commands that must be followed without question or effort.

With these practice commands, remember to use a downward intonation, and either drop or raise your volume level just a touch. Practice using them in a normal conversation, and you will notice how well changing the tone of your voice for hypnotic persuasion really works. Here are some basic commands that you can practice with:

"Would you like to go get some coffee, with me now?" (Take the intonation down on "with me now")

"Come with me."

"Let's go to the..." (Insert a place)

"Could you get that for me?" (Take the intonation down on "get that for me")

"Do you follow what I am saying?"

Yes, this is easy, but it works. Make sure that you only change your tone very slightly, so that it is barely perceptible, because this will be picked up by the subconscious mind while not being noticed by the person you are giving the commands to.

As you can see, using proper tonality is extremely important if you want to embed commands with your sentences. Obviously, everything in this book is important, but this is the very foundation of conversational hypnosis and should be mastered if you want to use covert hypnosis effectively.

When you practice using tonality to embed your commands on a daily basis, you easily build your hypnotic persuasion in a very short time, because this is extremely effective and simple.

To further build your hypnotic voice, and make your commands even more effective, you are always going to give a very slight pause before you give your commands. When you give a slight pause just before you give the command it actually holds the person you are talking to in slight suspense, so they listen more intently on what you are about to say, and their subconscious mind puts more emphasis on it.

The Complete Hypnotic Process

In order to persuade a person and get them to naturally follow your lead without question, you have to guide them in the proper sequence. The subsequent sequence is the precise hypnotic method that you use to get just about everyone to do as you say. This is the only hypnotic procedure that you need in order to successfully hypnotize a person. You can see for yourself just how easy it is.

1 - Grab their attention.

2 - Create states in the person of having an extraordinary connection with you. (Gain Rapport)

3 - Put them in the state(s) you want them in. (Like Excited!)

4 - Intensify and strengthen those states, and then link them to the action you want them to take.

Now, you can do this very easily, because it really is so simple, and it works. You can do it in as little as 1 to 5 minutes with as little as 3 or 4 sentences.

It is really important for you to understand how this hypnotic process, which you are doing, works. This is so you can make your own hypnotic strategies, points, and persuasion procedures easily because you know the process behind it. Make sense? It does when you think about it. Those people who only use the hypnotic points given in this book and mimic them (which will work a lot of the time) will not have the ability that you have to make your own hypnotic points; so, you will have the upper hand every time. When you fully understand this process, your persuasion abilities are surpassed by no other.

When you take the time and master the conversational hypnosis tactics in this book...

EVERYONE YOU SPEAK WITH WILL BE SO IMPRESSED BY YOU THAT THEY SHARE THEIR EXPERIENCES THAT THEY HAVE WITH YOU WITH OTHERS, AND FETCH YOU A CONSISTENTLY GROWING MOUNTAIN OF OPPORTUNITIES, AND YOU WILL END UP INFLUENCING THE OTHERS TOO! THE CYCLE CONTINUES.

Let us go over a quick example of a first time meeting so that you can see how easy this can be. I have put the subconscious hypnotic commands in bold:

"Hello, I am interested in social interactions and how they are influenced by subconscious bonds between people, like us, so I have to ask you a question. Have you ever instantly felt like you knew someone you just met? You know, possibly you just, **begin to have a connection with this person and instinctively know that you can trust them** and you might just **feel like you can like them and be good friends** because the subconscious bond is so powerful that you **completely feel attracted to this person**. It is really amazing and kind of funny because even though you just met this person you **feel extremely secure**, you **feel completely at ease**, and you **say to yourself, "I don't know why, but I really have to get know you now."** It is so exciting and it feels so good to **make that type of connection. Now, with me**, when I get this feeling I just can't help it. It is just a gut feeling that I can't explain, but it is cool because **you can simply let it happen**

33

immediately with this person because you know. It is an amazing encounter to have. You know what I mean?"

You can then just laugh and go on with normal conversation. It seems strange, but it works. If for some reason someone is not responsive, you can easily just move on. It gets easier with practice.

Trance States

In order to increase your success rate at effectively using conversational hypnosis to influence anyone, you can easily utilize the techniques in this chapter to force another person into a trance state. Putting someone into a trance state makes them more open to suggestion so that you can even more easily influence them to do as you wish.

So what is a trance state? A trance state is an altered state of consciousness, or any condition really, which is significantly different from a normal, waking, beta wave state. It is often experienced as daydreaming or intense concentration. Have you ever been so focused on something (TV especially) that everything else was completely ignored? Most likely you have experienced staring out the window in a classroom and completely lost track of what the teacher was saying. Every time you read a book you are interested in, like this one, you are going into a trance state. When any of these things happen, you have entered a trance state. This is extremely useful for you, because you can use it to your advantage when you put others into a trance state at will.

All of us enter trance states many times all throughout the day, and it is a time when our subconscious mind is extremely open to suggestion.

In order to force people into trance states, so that they will be more open to your hypnotic suggestions, you will need to change their state of consciousness. This is very easily done, so don't worry. The ways to put people into trance states are infinite, so you will learn just a couple here that are proven to work. When you try them out on your own you will see how well they work and know that these trance inducing methods are really effective, so you can learn more if you like; but you don't need to.

Covert hypnotic pattern interrupts are the simplest ways to put someone into a momentary trance state. Anytime that you interrupt a person's state of mind they have to actually go inside of their thought process to figure out where they were when you interrupted them. This now creates a sort of blank spot in the brain that can be filled. When you think about it, you understand that it is true. This is exciting!

The most famous hypnotic interrupt induction is the handshake interrupt used by the notorious Milton Erickson. The handshake interrupt is simply interrupting the process of a handshake, which causes a momentary blank in the brain, and then bringing the subjects hand up to their face, whilst using hypnotic NLP language to bring them into a trance state. This is not very covert, and is not normally what we use with conversational hypnosis. You will learn easier ways to covertly bring people into mild trance states using the conversational hypnosis techniques in this book.

A more covert hypnotic interrupt, which you can use in everyday conversation, is simply interrupting the person's you are hypnotizing sentence. You will find this to be very useful because it can be successfully used every day with anyone and you won't get caught.

All of your sentences are formed in your mind before you actually speak them. Imagine that you are the individual talking. You could think of a sentence right now, begin to say it; and if I were to interrupt you right in the middle of your sentence that you had already formed in your mind, your thoughts would go blank for a moment. This blank space is full of opportunities for me to put anything I like in there like, "you really like me." Do you see how simple this is? Yes, it works and you can use it on anyone.

A good example:

Individual talking: "So, I was reading this really good book and I thought…" you interrupt: "I really love this person (as you point to yourself), I'm just joking around. Go on with what you were saying."

The individual talking will probably laugh and continue with what they were saying before. You can be rest assured that it has worked.

Following are some dialogue stoppers that you can use to put people into mild trances, and then easily embed a command into their subconscious mind while they are trying to figure it out – or you can use them to just gain a minute to think about what you want to say next.

> Why would you think of something that isn't believable when it is?

> Why are you agreeing with this when you know it is true?

> The less you try the more you will agree.

> Are you aware of what you remember?

> What actually happens when a thought is formed?

> You can master anything that you pretend to.

> Just because I understand fully what you are saying does not make it true.

Do you still think what you believe you once thought?

Your response tells it all, even what you are unaware of.

You think this is great, but could you say it if you were unaware?

How do you stop a thought once you get it?

Your question is exactly what you wanted it to be, right?

Why are asking me what you don't actually understand really?

When you use one of these conversation stoppers, you will then immediately follow it with a command or statement that goes straight to the subconscious mind and is followed without question like:

"Why would you think of something that isn't believable when it is? Obviously, **this is believable**, easy to follow and **you love it**; but I was just wondering if you were paying attention to how cool this is. You know it is cool when both of us agree that **this is cool**. I know it is a bit confusing, but **you don't have to think about it** for it to be true, but **it is true**." Now, you can just laugh because it is fun, and they will laugh too because it is easier to just laugh than to think so hard about what was said.

Trick Phrases

Conversational hypnosis is the skill of effectively embedding commands in your speech so that a person's subconscious mind picks it up and obeys; however, the person does not catch on consciously to what you are doing because it appears to be normal conversation. In this particular section of the book, you are learning some hypnotic or "trick" phrases that you can use in your conversations to ease a person into a hypnotic command without them realizing it.

Remember, the formula for all hypnotic process is **a precise set of words (trick phrases), followed by an action verb that presumes you (the person you are talking to), and then the hypnotic command.** I will give you an example and break it down for you here:

Precise set of words - aka hypnotic phrase - aka trick phrase: *When you*

Action Verb: *Feel an urge to*

Hypnotic Command: *Practice*

Together we have the hypnotic phrase, "When you feel an urge to practice." Used in a sentence it is, "It is pretty easy, when you **feel an urge to practice**, to **learn conversational hypnosis**." The hypnotic suggestions for you to follow are in bold. This sentence may have two suggestions that a person can easily follow if you wanted to because it states, "*feel an urge to practice*" and "*learn conversational hypnosis*". Another example is, "When you **feel an urge to practice**, do you need to **act on that urge**?" Again, if I were to put the right hypnotic persuasion on this sentence it could easily have two commands to follow, "When you *feel an urge to practice*, do you need to *act on that urge*?" Do you see how easy this is? Yes, most things that work really well are easy when you break them down. It is a trick when things appear hard, because really they are easy. That is the secret.

After you finish reading this chapter, practice a few times, and you are getting the hang of using hypnotic phrases in you sentences; you will see, when you make your own, how it easy it is.

This is really easy to do, and just takes a little bit of thought. All you have to do is: simply think of the action that you want the person you are influencing to take, start off with a trick phrase, and then describe the course or experience towards the outcome you are influencing them to take. When you stir up and use their emotions to get them to take this action, they cannot help but follow because they are so excited.

The reason that these are considered "trick phrases" is because they tell the person to feel compelled to take action without appearing to do so. These phrases melt away any resistance that a person may have because it does not appear like you are actually directly commanding them, even though you are.

Some of these trick phrases work because they presuppose that the person is already taking the action. Others work because they appear to be a command about another person all together, while at the same time telling the subconscious mind of the person you are talking to that you are giving a command to them.

As you can see in the following examples, it is not as confusing as it appears to be. On the contrary it is really quite clear once you get a few of these down.

We will use each one of these trick phrases to embed the command, "*feel driven to rehearse*", for example, "**When you** *feel driven to rehearse* each of these trick phrases, can you help but master conversational hypnosis?"

When you… This assumes that the person is going to do the experience described. It is very powerful when you

39

follow this with a question because it puts the focus on the question, however it can be followed with a statement if done correctly like, "When you feel driven to rehearse all of the exercises in this book, you will be amazed at how easy it is to influence others!"

Similar Examples:

-While you

-If you

-Once you

-After you

An individual can… By talking about another person all together it makes it seem like you are not giving the person you are talking to a command when you really are. This destroys any resistance that they may have since you really aren't talking about them. "An individual can feel driven to rehearse this when they are reading something that they truly appreciate!"

Similar Examples:

-A person can

-Many people

-Most people

You don't have to… Since you are saying that they don't have to there is no pressure for them to take action. This phrase easily melts away all resistance. "You don't have to feel driven to rehearse; it is ok if you enjoy it."

Similar Examples:

-You really shouldn't

-Try not to

-Don't

-I'm not really sure if you

How amazed would you be to...? This implies that it is going to happen; the real question is about how amazed you are going to be when it does happen. "How amazed would you be to find that you feel driven to rehearse often all the exercises found in this book?"

Similar Examples:

-What would it be like to?

-How would you feel if?

You might discovery... "You might discover" is a great phrase to use when you have a bunch of actions that follow. This phrase implies that that you are going to experience what comes next without being told to experience it. It is great because it melts away all resistance with ease. "You might discover that when feel driven to rehearse, it can easily lead to you learning a lot from this; which is really exciting!"

-You may notice

-You can find

-It is interesting to notice

Are you starting to feel driven to rehearse yet? If you are that is ok, you can still practice and enjoy yourself as you read over the following examples. Just remember that these trick phrases work when you use them on anyone because they easily melt away any resistance that a person has to enjoying taking action.

Following are some more examples you can use that work great. You can use the following presuppositions as they are, or you can mix and match them. Add a verb to them like "feel", and then throw in a specific action you want the person to take; and you will have a hypnotic sentence that can not be beat. String a few of these sentences together

41

and incorporate them into normal conversation to complete the process. For example, "Well, you may find yourself feeling good as you read this because you are learning a ton; but if you already understand conversational hypnosis, and just come back to this guide from time to time as reference, that is ok too, because when you continuously study the methods in this guide, and others like it, you can't help but learn more."

While you…

As you…

When you…

Find yourself…

You might…

It's like you're…

You could (certainly, easily, quickly, etc.)…

A person (can, could, should, etc.)…

Some people can…

I like how you…

It just makes sense to…

I invite you to (notice, realize, picture, imagine, etc.)…

I don't know how you…

Would you ever…?

Some people (can, could, should, etc.)…

I'm (curious, wondering, etc.) if you…?

Have you ever…?

How would you…?

What would it be like if…?

Can you imagine...?

How do you...?

Could you...?

Do you think it's possible that...?

Don't you...?

Aren't you...?

Would you be (curious, surprised, excited, etc.) to know that...?

What will you do when...?

Are you (curious, surprised, excited, etc.)...?

Who would...?

What is it that...?

If you were to...?

You shouldn't...

If you could...?

Try not to...

You don't have to...

It's not necessary to...

I wouldn't tell you to...

You can't...

Don't... (think, say, feel, hear, etc.)

You won't...

You aren't...

When you add the above phrases to the hundreds of verbs you can use like "feel", and then throw in an action verb – you can easily make great hypnotic phrases of your own.

You can find hundreds of verbs here:
http://www.momswhothink.com/reading/list-of-verbs.html

The Most Important Chapter - Hypnotic Points

After you read this chapter you will see why it is the most important chapter in this book. These are the psychological devices (which I like to call hypnotic points) that you will use in order to create a hypnotic language pattern. Many people have just memorized and used these psychological devices with great success, but since you read this book, practiced the techniques in the previous chapters, have a deeper understanding of the way that the mind works and of all the little things that go into the hypnotic process; you will have a much better success rate when using these hypnotic points in your daily conversational hypnosis escapades.

Think about it: you know that people want to be lead and that you can easily become that leader, you have learned how to build rapport, you understand how to soften people up and let down their guard, you know the basic hypnotic formula, you have built and continue to work on your hypnotic voice, you have learned the complete hypnotic process, you know how to put people into trance states, and now you are learning the psychological devices that ensure that **you are a hypnotic powerhouse**. You already have enough hypnotic techniques in your arsenal to be more persuasive than 80% of the population. Once you have mastered these hypnotic language patterns, you will be unstoppable.

Even if you have skipped through the rest of this book and just memorize these hypnotic points to use on others, you will have a lot of success! That is how powerful this is.

You will find, as you continue reading, just how cool these psychological devices are because once you know them you can not only use them on others, but you will also be able to recognize when others are trying to use them on you. The beauty is that most people who use them do not even know what they are doing. They just learned how to "sell" themselves, or something else, to others. You will have much more power because you understand what is actually going on, and so you can easily render their attempts at persuading you useless. You can then run through the tremendous amount of hypnotic points that you have learned in this book, and influence them! They won't know what hit them.

Are you excited yet? Yes! If you are, that is ok – because these hypnotic points are so powerful that, once you use them, you have tremendous power over others anyway! Just practice and you can see how well they work for yourself. So let us get started.

Hypnotic Point #1 - Presuppositions

Presuppositions are basic assumptions that something is fact when it really may not be. We all have them do to our own experiences, opinions, and personal beliefs. Life would be impossible to live if we did not have these basic assumptions because, among other things, we could not learn from our mistakes and successes. Presuppositions are neither good nor bad; they are just assumptions that are made. So it is best to just treat them as such, if you want to have power over them.

Do you think that you will learn anything after you are done reading this entire book if you did not assume that you can learn in the first place? Learning is possible because you assume that you can. The presupposition in everyday conversation is often disguised, but after you read this, and practice it, you will be able to spot it a mile away. The presupposition in the first sentence of this paragraph is that you will read this book. It is a bit disguised, but "after you are done reading this entire book" presupposes that you will read this entire book. Which may be true, but there is no evidence that supports that statement.

Maybe you can now see how powerful presuppositions can be. They are very powerful to use in conversational hypnosis because you can easily put them into your sentences to tell another person, subconsciously, to assume that they are already doing what you want them to do.

When you fully understand presuppositions, you can also use this knowledge to your defense. A lot of questions that people ask have presuppositions in them. "Why can't we just talk without arguing?" presupposes that you can't talk with that person without arguing. If you were to try to answer that question directly, you would be making a serious mistake because obviously you do not always argue. If you tried to say something like, "We don't always argue." you would be arguing and invalidating the person's feelings. If you try to answer that question directly with any answer, you would be lost before you even begun. I would respond to that question with something like, "I am sorry that you felt we always argued before, but I am open to talking right now, without arguing. Let's just talk without arguing and see how well we do. OK?" You can see that that answer has a lot of hypnotic points in it, but let's just focus, for now, on the fact that it is not directly answering the question; which successfully deflates the question, and brings the control of the conversation back to its proper place.

Presuppositions are very powerful, and come in many different forms; which allows you to use them in all of your conversations with great success. It is extremely hard to get caught using them, and usually *the person you are talking to always does what you say without any opposition* because they would rather someone outside themselves make decisions for them anyway. After you have been practicing using them with success you know exactly what I mean and understand how powerful they are.

Use It With Questions:

One very powerful way that you can use presuppositions in your everyday conversation is with questions. This may actually be a little more difficult than using presuppositions with direct commands, but it is still really easy to do, so you are learning this first.

Presupposing using questions is often used by salesman. They may say things like, "Which insurance would you rather have the next time you get into an accident?" That question presupposes that you are going to get into an accident. It also presupposes that you are getting insurance because it asks you, and seems to give you a choice between, which one you would rather have. Most people will not even ask, even to themselves, why the insurance salesman thinks they are going to get into an accident, or why they think that they are definitely getting insurance. The images that this question usually brings about are ones of getting into an accident. A person will normally begin to vividly imagine an accident happening, and want to get "good insurance" to protect themselves, and will look to the insurance salesman to tell them which insurance is best.

If you watch TV, the next time you do, pay attention to the commercials and you will see how often this technique is used. It is used all the time because it works extremely well. You don't have to watch TV in order to see this technique used successfully in advertisements, because it is used in all advertising in every platform.

47

Here are some quick examples:

The question "Which credit card is right for you?" followed by a list of credit cards presupposes that one of the following credit cards is right for the person and forces them to decide which one.

The statement and question, "before you begin your shopping, are you going to be using cash or credit to make your purchases?" forces the person to choose between which form of payment they are going to make when they make a purchase, presupposing that they are shopping and are going to make a purchase.

"What kind of car are you looking to buy here today?" presupposes that the person is going to buy a car, there, and today.

As you can see in the examples above: sometimes the questions are double questions that force the person to make a choice, and sometimes they are just questions that redirect the attention away from the presupposition that they are following, which is your suggestion. This is so fun, isn't it? Of course it can be if you have fun with it.

Here are some more examples to help you along:

"Would you like to forgive me now, or do you want to wait to forgive me until directly after I told you what I did?"

"What will you do when the police arrest you for drinking and driving?"

"If you did want to, why would you want to quit smoking?"

"What is it about this book that you find so interesting?"

"Do you like the knowledge you are gaining best or is it the fun you are having?"

"Would you rather me take you out on an official date or would you rather I just take you to eat somewhere for fun?"

"When was the last time you had so much fun?"

Do you understand how powerful this psychological device can be when you use it correctly? Yes, I did use a bit of presupposition in my question there, but it is only obvious to the very few who know; most people will just do as you say without question when you use this awesome psychological device.

Self-Defense:

Now that you can spot presupposing questions a mile away; to defend against them and render them powerless, you can easily just ask the question, "What makes you think I am going to do that?" or "What makes you think that that is the way it is?" For example, in the first example about forgiveness, you could say, "What makes you think I am going to forgive you?" These questions will put the pressure back on them, giving you time to formulate what to do next. You can also make a statement like, "I may think about doing that (whatever it is) later, but right now I just need to use your bathroom, and after that I will come and get you if I want you, so could you please just point me in the direction of your bathroom? Thanks!" Saying something like this completely derails them and gives you time to think.

Make Presupposing Statements:

When you make presupposing statements, with your command embedded in them, it is often just as powerful as presupposing questions. Sometimes it is more powerful. I will teach you exactly how to do this very easily. Here is an extremely powerful formula for making presuppositions that will work for you most of the time:

You give a simple fact, followed by an adverb or two like "so" or "obviously", and then follow with your command that goes directly into the subconscious mind.

It is so easy! Here is an example: *You are reading this now. So, obviously you are learning a lot about conversational hypnosis.*

Fact – You are reading this now.

Adverb – So, and obviously.

Command for you to follow – you are learning a lot about conversational hypnosis.

Now, you can see that I used the words "so" and "obviously", and that is perfectly ok because it still works when you use more than one. This psychological device is extremely powerful because it is a fact that you are reading this now, but to whom is it so obvious that you are learning a lot about conversational hypnosis? You also may learn it better when you actually practice it, not necessarily when you just read about it.

If you think about it, you can see that the example above is not logical, it just sounds logical. This is so simple and it works great, which is why it is such a powerful form of conversational hypnosis!

Here are some words that you can use when you make your own presuppositions using that extremely powerful formula:

Apparently, certainly, clearly, definitely, distinctly, evidently, incontestably, noticeably, of course, openly, plainly, seemingly, surely, undeniably, undoubtedly, unquestionably, visibly, without doubt, unmistakably, so, absolutely, beyond any doubt, categorically, decidedly, doubtless, doubtlessly, easily, explicitly, expressly, far and away, finally, indubitably, no ifs ands or buts about it, positively, specifically, unequivocally, without fail, without question.

And some more not so obvious ones:

Objectively, suddenly, naturally, actually, ethically, now, normally, however, shortly, again, think about it, you see, anyway, since, when, if, be aware, realize, come to the conclusion, ignore.

Here are some examples of how these can be used:

Apparently, you are learning conversational hypnosis by reading this.

Certainly, you are having fun!

You are still reading. Clearly, you are getting it.

You are reading this, so you are definitely getting it.

Objectively, it is the truth – you just have to practice.

Suddenly, you may find yourself having fun using conversational hypnosis.

Naturally, you will have to practice before you get real good!

Actually, it is quite easy when you think about it.

Ethically, you have nothing to worry about because you are doing this to benefit everyone.

Self-Defense:

Once again, you can easily defend against presuppositions and render them powerless – now that you can spot them a mile away. Just ask the right questions like, "What makes you think I am going to do that?" or "What makes you think that that is the way it is?"

Using the examples shown, here is something that you can say to combat:

Apparently, you are learning conversational hypnosis by reading this.

What makes you think I am learning anything? Who is that apparent to?

Certainly, you are having fun!

What makes you think I am having fun? Why are you so certain?

You are still reading. Clearly, you are getting it.

Getting what?

You see, now that you are getting it, conversational hypnosis is really fun when you think about it because you know the secrets to making it fun for everyone! Can you see why I have so much fun with this? Yes, presuppositions are one of my favorite hypnotic tools because they are so darn simple yet powerful to use, and hardly anyone ever notices you using them.

Some More Tricky Presuppositions

Presuppositions are so widely used that they are sometimes hard to spot unless you understand them and know what to look for. But, once you do, it can seem as though you are a mind reader because you know how to read in between the lines and understand what people are truly saying.

Let's see if you can spot the hidden messages in these examples of simple presuppositions:

When you continue to read… presupposes you are going to continue to read.

Ignore any preconceived notions… presupposes you had preconceived notions about something.

So, how will you feel... presupposes that you are going to feel something.

Naturally, this will cause you to... presupposes that this is going to cause you to do something.

Come to the conclusion... presupposes that you are going to come to a conclusion.

Ok, so those are pretty easy for you to spot now that you understand, but I can tell you for sure that most people do not spot them, and will easily be influenced by such devices.

Let's try a few more that are a bit trickier:

You are as determined as your father. - By now you can see that this is presupposing that you are determined, but this also presupposes that your father is determined too.

You'll understand when you grow up. - Obviously, this is presupposing that the person doesn't understand now and will understand when grown. But, it is also presupposing that the person is not grown up yet.

I won't be fooled again. - Have you been fooled before?

That is so gay. - Sadly, I have heard this one quite often. Is it really a bad thing to be gay?

Why don't you laugh more? - I don't laugh enough?

I regret not studying more in school. - I suppose this person went to school, did not study enough, regrets it, wishes that they knew more now, feels a bit bad about themselves, wants to feel better about themselves now, wants help, and is looking to learn something. There is a lot of presuppositions in this little statement. A little more probing will show me exactly what will motivate them to take action now. This is precisely why it may seem like you are reading minds now that you understand presuppositions.

53

Self-Defense:

Remember, understanding and spotting presuppositions is the hardest part. Now that you can do that, all you have to do to render them powerless is ask a simple question like: "What makes you think that…?" Replacing the dots (…) with the presupposition. Like, "What makes you think I am not grown up?" or "What makes you think I do not understand now?" See how easy it is? Yes, a person really can have a ton of fun with this when they practice, because it is extremely easy and it works well.

Hypnotic Point #2 - Unspecified Nouns

All sentences have a subject that is supplied by a noun. The subject is what the sentence is about. When the subject of the sentence is not well defined it is known as an unspecified noun. For example, "he went to the store" is a sentence that uses an unspecified noun because "he" is not well defined. We do not know who "he" is unless the person is pointing to "he" when it is said. "I went to the store" uses a specified noun because we know that the subject is me.

Here are some more sentences using highlighted unspecified nouns to make it clearer for you:

"**They** think I am cute." *Who does?*

"**He** gets it." *Who is he?*

"**That** is annoying." *What is that?*

Any noun that is used without a specific subject is an unspecified noun. In order to clear up any confusion when someone else is using unspecified nouns in their sentences, just ask the questions who or what specifically (like I have in *italics* in the previous examples).

You can use this to your benefit when using conversational hypnosis by using unspecified nouns to confuse the listener before leading their thoughts. When you generalize your nouns while you are talking to someone they are going to be so caught up in trying to figure out what you mean, because you are leaving out specific information that they need in order to follow what you are saying - you can begin to lead their thoughts towards whatever you deem fit.

In other words, when you use unspecified nouns, the person you are talking to is focusing their energy on trying to figure out who or what you are talking about. While they are doing this you can make it easier on them by filling in the blanks, moving on and embedding some commands into what you say next. Now, remember that you have to speak hypnotically while using conversational hypnosis and embedding commands.

Here is an example of using unspecified nouns, with the commands you want followed in bold:

Imagine you just came back to your date with 2 drinks and while handing one to them you laugh and say, "They think I am charming, well, most people **think I am charming** because when they **listen to me speak,** you can **simply find it delightful**, and **smile - it's really charming** - well, that's what they just said anyway, how interesting." (And smile then laugh some more)

As you can see, this starts out with a sentence that includes the unspecified noun "they", and immediately it is clarified that "they" is most people followed by the command "think I am charming." With this hypnotic paragraph you can see how easy it is to use unspecified nouns in order to turn a normal conversation into conversational hypnosis that you can use to easily influence anyone without them knowing it.

The hypnotic process that you will use unspecified nouns in is easy. Say a sentence or phrase with an unspecified noun in it and right at the point that they begin to question exactly who or what you mean, give them the answer followed by an embedded command. You can continue with a few more embedded commands in order to make sure that their subconscious is doing exactly what you want without conscious intervention.

Here is the hypnotic process using unspecified nouns again:

You make a phrase with an unspecified noun in it -> they think to ask you a question to clarify what you mean -> you answer it for them before they ask and deliver you embedded commands.

This will always work for you when you do it correctly. Even when they just look at you and say "huh?" you know that it worked because their subconscious mind has picked it up. You can change the subject and move on.

Go ahead and practice the above hypnotic point on anyone and you will see how powerful it is. If you say the exact sentence above using your hypnotic voice, pausing slightly, and embedding your commands; you will know for yourself how well it works. Go ahead and replace the word "charming" with interesting, funny, silly, witty, or whatever you like. It may take some practice, but it will be worth it when it works and the people you converse with can't get enough of you. They may even begin to talk about you when you are not there because you are so interesting to them.

This is conversational hypnosis and hypnotic point #2. When you practice this daily you will be amazed at how well it works. Anyone you have a conversation with will talk about you and bring you more and more favorable circumstances, and you will end up seducing, charming, and influencing them too!

Hypnotic Point #3 - Unspecified Verbs

I bet that you can guess that this is the same as unspecified nouns, except that you are using verbs instead of nouns. It is, it works just as well and is just as easy. If you want to clarify unspecified verbs, all you have to do is question "how" "when" and/or "where" specifically.

Examples:

"She helped me." *How did she help you? When? Where?*

"Change the laundry." *How should I change it? When? Where?*

"I tried to fix it!" *How did you try to fix it? When? Where?*

"Go on a date with me." *How should I go with you? Where should we go? When?*

When you make a statement with an unspecified verb in it, logically, the person will ask themselves "how precisely?" which is your chance to answer that question immediately and begin to embed your commands that they will gladly follow.

For example: "Do you want to **go on another date with me**? When you do you could **choose the place to go** that will make you **feel real good about it**, and I could pick you up if it makes you **feel comfortable,** so if you want to **make plans now**, with me, and you want to **go on another date with me,** just **choose the place to go, now** and I will pick you up tomorrow about 6:00pm. Where do **you want to go**?"

Imagine that you were on a date with this person and it has been going great! When you ask your question like this, embed the commands that are in bold with your hypnotic voice, pause slightly, and then explain to them exactly how to answer you by choosing the place to go; they will most likely just tell you where they want to go because you have made everything else easy for them.

This is hypnotic point #3 and, of course, when you practice using it you will see how well it works. This is a great one to use with kids or employees because you can tell them exactly how to do what you want them to do right now, how easy it is, and the reward they will get if they do it right now. Practice it and you will know exactly what I mean.

Hypnotic Point #4 - Cause and Effect

I can only assume that now, after you have been reading and practicing conversational hypnosis, you are noticing more about language patterns, and how powerful hypnotic effect is when used correctly. You may have noticed that it is used in all forms of advertising, and especially by those in power. One of the most influential forms of communication is saturated with terms of cause and effect. This is important to understand if you want to use one of the easiest hypnotic points to use. Cause and effect is indeed easy to use and works great.

You may hear people speak in terms of cause and effect all of the time. Anytime you hear someone say something like, "You make me feel..." or "That bores me", they are speaking in terms of cause and effect. The first example "you" is the cause and "make me feel something" is the effect. Of course, you know that in the second example the cause is "that" and "bores me" is the effect.

Those examples show us exactly how easily the majority of the population will accept statements as logical when they really might not be. Nothing and nobody can ever really make a person feel or do anything. We always have choice.

You know this, but obviously most people do not and will gladly accept something that you say as the logical truth if you say it in terms of cause and effect.

It is usually not necessary to question others when they are using cause and effect in their language patterns because they will, more often than not, just get annoyed by you. I know from experience. But it is really easy to question it in your head, just so that you know exactly what the truth is. The way that you do this is easy, just follow along and ask yourself exactly how one thing causes the other.

Unless you are really trying to change the way a person thinks, you do not need to question people directly when they use cause and effect statements. When someone says "He makes me angry", you can say something like, "how precisely do you make yourself feel angry at something he is doing or saying?" Obviously, this can really make matters worse; which is why it is not usually necessary to question it except in your own head so that you understand what is really going on. It is up to you.

Using cause and effect to persuade others is really easy; you just have to put words into your sentences like "because, causing, causes, cause, etc." For instance, "Because you are still reading this book, you must be learning all about conversational hypnosis." That statement seems logical, but it is not necessarily true. Are you learning? Yes, this may be true, but it is not necessarily a fact that is caused by reading this book. Does reading this book necessarily cause you to learn? It does not. Only you can cause you to learn.

Another thing is that this book may contain everything that you *need* to know about conversational hypnosis in order to use it successfully to persuade anyone, but, it couldn't possibly cover everything there is to know about the subject; so, is it even possible to learn all about it just because you are still reading this book? Clearly, this cause and effect statement is a really good example, but it can be misleading if you didn't know about cause and effect.

Do you see how powerful using this psychological device is? Yes, you may, but you will know it for sure, positively, without a doubt after you practice a few times. When you make statements in terms of cause and effect, they seem very true and logical, even if they are not.

Now that you understand cause and effect, if you continue reading, you will be amazed at how much your influence over others grows. When you practice this hypnotic point daily, your conversational hypnosis skills will grow tremendously, and, obviously, your influence over others will too.

Hypnotic Point #5 - Comparisons and Judgments

The statement "The new and improved liquid detergent is simply better." is a comparison that is not clear on purpose. What is it better than? Is it better than it was before? Is it better than other detergents? Is it better than not using detergents before? Is it better because it is liquid? You could also ask, "How is it improved?" As you can see, that statement sounds very logical and true, even if it isn't.

Here is an example of a judgment: "The new and improved liquid detergent is the best detergent you can buy!" Who says? Judgments are easy to spot because they are stating and opinion as a fact.

Judgments are very often used with comparisons which is why they are both included here under one hypnotic point. They are very similar in the way that they are used and defended against.

Both comparisons and judgments can be very cleverly disguised and justified by using the word "because". When you use the word "because" after one of these statements followed by a reason, most the time people will accept what you say as logical and true.

For example: "This book is one of the best books that you can get on the subject of conversational hypnosis because no other book comes close to the quality and ease of use for the price. When you compare it, you will notice the difference for yourself, obviously a lot of work went into it. You can see for yourself how easy it is to persuade others once you read it because it gives you all the tools you need."

When you are making a comparison it is better to immediately begin to explain why it is better than what you are comparing it to because if you put the emphases on "why", then it takes the minds attention away from the what. More than likely, people are going to be more interested in why it is better than what it is you are comparing it to. To do this simply say, "because" and then continue with an explanation. When you do this, other people will believe it is better because you gave them a reason why it is.

When you are making a judgment it is a really good idea to immediately begin to explain why your judgment is right in order to seemingly prove that it is right. To do this simply say, "because" and then continue with an explanation. When you do this, other people will believe your judgment is true because you gave them an explanation why it is.

Self-Defense:

Judgments and comparisons can be made clear and defended against by asking who it is that is making the judgment, what is it being compared to, and on what grounds are these statements made.

61

Hypnotic Point #6 - Nominalization

Nominalization refers to the use of a verb or an adjective as a noun. If a noun is used in a sentence and cannot be touched, tasted, seen, or smelt; it is a nominalization. The use of nominalization can be very useful in your conversations because they are usually quite vague, and always have very different meanings for everyone. Let's look at an example sentence with italicized nominalizations:

Concentration and *willpower*, utilized with *enthusiasm* and *persistence* are *necessities* if you want *success*.

As you can see, there are a lot of nominalizations in that sentence. The sentence is perfectly structured and contains no grammatical errors. At first glance, it appears to make complete sense; but at closer look, we can find that it needs a lot more clarifying. Let's break it down a bit more for clarity:

What does the word "concentration" mean in this sentence? Whose concentration are we talking about? How are they concentrating? What are they concentrating on? How are they using their concentration?

If this supposed noun were an actual person, place, or thing we would know exactly what it was. In order to understand what this nominalization means, we would have to ask a lot more questions.

What does the word "success" mean in this sentence? Success in what? Who is having this success that I might want? What is the success effecting?

Do you understand how confusing and vague nominalizations really are? Yes, they can be very useful if you are selling something to someone, but they shouldn't be used otherwise. Politicians and salesman use nominalizations all of the time because they confuse the listener into believing that they are saying something that is important, when they are really saying something that does not mean anything at all.

If you break down the example sentence and try to understand what it means, you will find that, even though it sounds logical, it has no real meaning at all. This sentence might be used by a politician, salesman, teacher, boss or someone else who is trying to motivate others to do something.

Nominalizations delete so much information out of sentences, are very corrupting to an individual's mind, and should not be used because they are already used way to much as it is, and it is difficult enough trying to keep track of them all without anyone adding any more.

Even though it is not a good idea to use nominalizations when you are using conversational hypnosis to persuade others, they are often used in advertising and political speeches, in order to confuse the listener, because it is very difficult for a person to try and figure out what is being said, so they just accept it as the truth.

Even though you won't be using nominalizations to persuade others, it is very important to understand and spot nominalizations so that you can clarify and defend against them when they are being used.

Self-Defense:

Now that you know how important it is for you to understand and spot nominalizations, you just have to defend against them by turning them into verbs and asking for the missing information. "Who is concentrating on what, and how are they doing it?"

Hypnotic Point #7 - Linguistic Binds

Once you finish this chapter, you will know that linguistic binds are very simple, yet extremely powerful. When you use a linguistic bind, the listener thinks that what you say is absolutely true; they have no question about it, believe you completely, and just do as you say.

It is really easy to make your own linguistic binds; merely state a fact that is obvious and then follow it with your command.

For example: "Now that you have been reading this book, you can begin to understand how powerful conversational hypnosis is, especially when you use this information on others to get them to do anything you want."

You can also use a linguistic bind by saying, "the more you A, the more you B."

For example: "The more you read, the more you understand."

When you use linguistic binds you are causing a person to believe that what you are saying is very logical and true even though it is not. The second part of the first sentence, even though it may be true, does not follow the first part of the sentence logically. The fact is that you have been reading this book (at least partially). I follow that fact with a command that you can easily follow: you can begin to understand how useful this book is when you use the information that you find in it, on others. For the second example, just because a person reads does not mean that they understand.

Do you see how powerful this is? Do you understand how you can use this psychological device to easily make anyone agree with everything you say? Yes, I am sure that you do because it just makes sense.

Hypnotic Point #8 - Modal Operators of Necessity

You can easily spot modal operators of necessity because they always indicate that you should or should not do something. Sometimes these statements are a little more forceful when they include words like must, must not, or don't. There are a lot of examples of these phrases in the chapter called, "trick phrases." These statements are easily clarified by asking what would happen if you did or did not do it?

Here are some examples:

You should always brush your teeth after every meal - *"What would happen if you didn't?"*

I shouldn't ever try that - *"What would happen if you did?"*

I must eat everything on my plate - *"What would happen if you didn't?"*

You ought not to do that - *"What would happen if you did?"*

Often times, these statements are for your own benefit; but, they can also be used negatively to limit the options available to you. The only way to know for sure is to critically evaluate what is being said and decide if it is beneficial to follow the advice or not. This can easily be done by asking what would happen if you did or did not do it?

It is also extremely important for you to always be careful in the words that you choose when you form your commands. Obviously, it is better to say, "You should drive carefully." instead of, "Don't get into an accident."

It is really easy for you to use these psychological devices when you are using conversational hypnosis to persuade others. When modal operators of necessity are used, the mind immediately begins to think of 2 things:

1-The topic being discussed - For example when I say, "Don't even think about going out with your friends, tonight." You probably are thinking about going out with your friends. You may be thinking about all your friends that will be there, the good music, the great food and drink. If you like going out with your friends, then this will be positive for you.

2-What would happen if the opposite is true? - By using the example above, you will most likely ask yourself, even if only subconsciously, "What would happen if I did go out with my friends?"

I am sure, by now you can see how powerful this can be when you are influencing others by using conversational hypnosis. If you want them to think about something that makes them feel really good you can just tell them that they don't need to think about it. You can follow that with your command. You can also easily answer the question of what would happen if the opposite is true, with a command.

Examples:

"You probably shouldn't think about your favorite food right now, it may make you hungry, and then you might just easily be persuaded to go out with me to get some food."

"Try not to think about using conversational hypnosis, it could cause you to realize how easy it is to influence others to do anything you want."

"You should refer back to this book, often, in order to keep up on your persuasion skills; but if you don't, that's ok, at least you can practice some of the techniques so you can see how powerful they are for yourself."

Hypnotic Point #9 - Modal Operators of Possibility

Modal operators of possibility are very similar to modal operators of necessity except that they deal with what is or isn't possible instead of what is or isn't necessary. For instance, it is impossible to walk through walls but it is possible to learn math. It is easy to spot modal operators of possibility because they include words like, "cannot, can't, impossible, and couldn't". These statements are easily clarified by asking what would happen if you did or did not do it, and what is preventing you from doing it?

I do not use modal operators of possibility on others because it is very limiting, can cause a very unpleasant reaction in the other person, and is therefore not a good method of persuasion. I only include them in this book so that you can recognize them and defend against them.

Even though it is not a good idea to use modal operators of possibility, if you wanted to, you can use them by influencing others that they aren't capable of doing something unless they use your product or services.

For example: "If you are like most people and struggling with weight loss, it is not your fault; you're just missing the biggest reason why *you can't lose weight*. The big companies don't want you to know this, but I have figured out how you can lose weight. By following the simple steps in my FREE REPORT you can see for yourself just how easy it is."

In the above sentence it clearly states that you can't lose weight unless you get the FREE REPORT. Obviously, this is clear to you, but it will easily trick most people. The only problem that you will have if you tell a person that they can't do something is that they will probably resent you for it in the long run. Unfortunately, I know from experience, and can tell you that no good comes out of it. It is much more beneficial to use all the other conversational hypnosis methods in this book to influence others. As long as you are benefiting them, you will always be able to influence others with ease, and they will always be happy doing as you wish.

Hypnotic Point #10 - Universal Quantifiers

All or nothing. That is what a universal quantifier is. When someone says, "I always get sick." they are using a universal quantifier. It is quite clear that they don't always get sick or else they would never be healthy. When a few instances are used to represent a whole group or period of time, it is a universal quantifier. "I think reading is boring" or "classical music sucks" are universal quantifiers. With universal quantifiers there are no exceptions.

Here are some more examples:

-"New cars have great motors"

-"All universal quantifiers are wrong"

-"I never get sick"

-"Every time I go out I get sunburned"

-"Indian food is spicy"

Universal quantifiers are rarely true, but they are not always wrong. They can be facts as well. The Earth is always spinning. If the Earth stopped spinning, then this would not be true, but for now this is a true universal quantifier. This is very different than, "I can't do anything right." Nobody can always do everything wrong. It is impossible.

It is easy to counter a universal quantifier with the question, "is there an instance when this is not the case?"

For example:

"I always fail at everything." *Was there ever a time when you succeeded at something? Did you successfully wake up this morning, or are you still sleeping?*

"Why am I always so depressed?" *Was there ever a time in your entire life when you were not depressed? Can you think about something that you enjoy doing? Do you have a favorite activity? Is there someone you enjoy being around?* These questions can lead to thoughts of happiness.

"Indian food is so spicy." *Have you ever had Indian rice pudding? It is sweet. Naan is often very plain.*

As you can see, it is very easy to spot universal quantifiers and find out their validity through simple questions.

Remember, successful people use universal quantifiers in a beneficial way. If you constantly say that you always succeed, you will. When you are communicating with others, it is a good idea to use universal quantifiers in a positive rather than negative way because people will appreciate you more. When people appreciate you more, you will have a much easier time influencing them.

Final Thoughts and Continued Study

If you have made it this far, and actually done the exercises in this book; you are now more persuasive than most of the world's population, and you definitely have all the conversational hypnosis tools you will ever need in order to succeed! I am sure that you have already experienced much success with your influence over others.

Just remember that, with any skill (including this one), you must practice in order to improve and keep it up. Keep practicing and you will experience unparalleled success!

Even though many people read this book over and over again, in order to absorb all there is to know about conversational hypnosis and improve their skills; and even though this book contains enough information to keep you more persuasive and far ahead of the majority of people - If you are like me, you will want to continue improving your skills and learning much more. I am always continuing my education and have come across some absolutely essential material on improving the craft. Here are some recommendations that you can use to improve your craft:

The Power of Conversational Hypnosis *by Igor Ledochowski:* This is by far the best and most in depth course you can get on the subject. It includes an audio course, manual, cheat sheets, tons of bonuses, and everything you can possibly think of to guarantee your success. You can get 3 superb sessions & manual completely FREE just for checking it out. This is the best and you can see it for yourself when you check it out. This is the best and you can see it for yourself when you visit his site: http://tinyurl.com/bu6ct7q.

Learn Hypnosis & Hypnotherapy from Beginner to Mastery: Becoming a Brief Therapist 'Special Edition the Complete Works Vol I-V *by Dan Jones*: This is really great because it is in another kindle book, which I love. It is also available in paperback if you would like to have it on your bookshelf. This book is very thorough and an asset to anyone who is serious in mastering the art of conversational hypnosis. You can find it on amazon here: http://amzn.to/U44y3e

One Last Thing

You have an opportunity to rate this book and share it with your friends on your facebook and twitter accounts. If you believe that your friends will benefit from this work, please share. I would be honored and very grateful.

Also, if you could please review this book on amazon, Barns and Nobles, Kobo, or wherever else you may have purchased it; it will help others like yourself gain the benefit that I sincerely hope this book has given you. I would be eternally thankful. Without reviews, this valuable information gets lost in the void.

Thank You,

All the best,

Michael

37436531R00049

Made in the USA
Lexington, KY
02 December 2014